MODERN ROLE MODELS

Matt Damon

Pamela D. Toler

Mason Crest Publishers

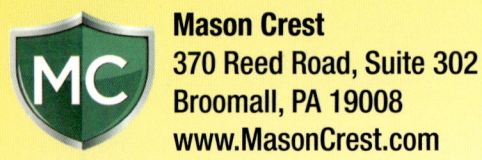

Mason Crest
370 Reed Road, Suite 302
Broomall, PA 19008
www.MasonCrest.com

Copyright © 2013 by Mason Crest, an imprint of National Highlights, Inc.

All rights reserved. No part of this publication may be reproduced or transmitted in any form or by any means, electronic or mechanical, including photocopying, recording, taping, or any information storage and retrieval system, without permission from the publisher.

Printed and bound in the United States of America

CPSIA Compliance Information: Batch #MRM2013. For further information, contact Mason Crest at 1-866-MCP-Book.

First Printing

1 3 5 7 9 8 6 4 2

Library of Congress Cataloging-in-Publication Data

Toler, Pamela D.
 Matt Damon / Pamela D. Toler.
   p. cm. — (Modern role models)
 Includes bibliographical references and index.
 ISBN 978-1-4222-2718-3 (hc)
 ISBN 978-1-4222-9090-3 (ebook)
1. Damon, Matt—Juvenile literature. 2. Motion picture actors and actresses—United States—Biography—Juvenile literature. I. Title.
 PN2287.D255T65 2013
 791.4302'8092—dc23
   [B]
                              2012037506

CROSS-CURRENTS

In the ebb and flow of the currents of life we are each influenced by many people, places, and events that we directly experience or have learned about. Throughout the chapters of this book you will come across CROSS-CURRENTS reference boxes. These boxes direct you to a CROSS-CURRENTS section in the back of the book that contains fascinating and informative sidebars and related pictures. Go on. ▶▶

Contents

1 **Honored with a Star**   5

2 **A Shared Dream**   11

3 **A Shooting Star**   17

4 **Back on the A-List**   27

5 **New Roles**   37

Cross-Currents   46

Chronology   56

Accomplishments & Awards   57

Further Reading & Internet Resources   59

Glossary   60

Notes   61

Index   63

Picture Credits   64

About the Author   64

Matt Damon was honored on July 25, 2007, with the 2,343rd star to be placed on the Hollywood Walk of Fame, in Los Angeles, California. The award was long overdue recognition of Matt's many accomplishments. This talented actor in both drama and comedy is also an award-winning writer and film and television producer.

Honored with a Star

IN THE SUMMER OF 2007, ACTOR MATT DAMON received one of Hollywood's biggest honors—a star on the Hollywood Walk of Fame. The unveiling of Matt's star took place on the same day that yet another of his blockbuster films, *The Bourne Ultimatum*, **PREMIERED** in Hollywood—the district in Los Angeles, California, that is the center of the U.S. movie industry.

➤ WALK OF FAME ➤

The Hollywood Walk of Fame is a three-and-a-half mile trail of 2,500 pink and bronze stars set in the sidewalk along Hollywood Boulevard and Vine Street in Hollywood. The star-studded sidewalk serves as a hall of fame for the best in the entertainment business. Each year since 1958, notable actors, singers, directors, and others are chosen by the Hollywood Chamber of Commerce to receive a sidewalk star in recognition of their contributions to the entertainment industry.

MATT DAMON

At the July 25, 2007, unveiling ceremony of Matt Damon's star, the 36-year-old actor was introduced by Paul Greengrass, director of *The Bourne Ultimatum*. He told the crowd that Matt deserved this honor because he truly was a star:

> "A star is not the same as being a celebrity. A star is being a great actor, an iconic actor, and a man graceful with fame. He's all of those things."

Then Matt came to the podium. As he looked out at hundreds of well-wishers, he admitted to feeling overwhelmed, saying:

> "A few times in my life I've had these experiences that are just kind of too big to process and this looks like it's going to be one of those times."

Matt went on to reminisce about how he had lived near the Walk of Fame as a young, struggling actor. He and his longtime friend and fellow aspiring actor Ben Affleck had often walked on the star-studded sidewalk, Matt told the crowd:

> "Ben and I lived in a really, really crappy apartment about five blocks away from here and we used to walk up and down here and look at these stars. . . . I hoped, I dreamed that this would happen."

Matt finished his remarks by thanking his mother for giving him life, his wife for giving him a beautiful stepdaughter and daughter, and the crowd for sharing the event with him. He paid tribute to his roots as well, noting that he also gave thanks that the Boston Red Sox—his hometown baseball team—were in first place.

⇒ Another Honor ⇐

The Walk of Fame starts just outside Grauman's Chinese Theater, the site of numerous star-studded film premieres dating from the 1920s. The theater features a cement block courtyard where over the years, people associated with the film industry have left autographs, handprints, footprints, or other impressions. Leaving a mark at Grauman's

Honored with a Star

is an honor that only about 200 people have been given since the theater opened in 1927.

A month before the unveiling of his star on the Walk of Fame, Matt and fellow actors George Clooney and Brad Pitt, as well as producer Jerry Weintraub, were invited to leave their footprints at Grauman's Chinese Theatre. Matt and the others came prepared to leave a big impression. Because they knew their concrete impressions would shrink when dry, all wore bigger shoes than usual. Matt told reporters at the ceremony,

CROSS-CURRENTS

To find out more about the site where famous Hollywood actors have left their mark over the years, read "Grauman's Chinese Theater." Go to page 46.

On May 24, 2007, Matt and costars Brad Pitt (left) and George Clooney (right) attended the world premiere of *Ocean's Thirteen*, at the Cannes Film Festival, in France. Soon afterward the three costars would leave their footprints in wet concrete at Grauman's Chinese Theater—an honor that has been bestowed on only about 200 people in the entertainment industry.

MATT DAMON

> "George told me people were going to look at our footprints forever, so we gotta size up."

ALL THE WAY TO THE BANK

According to the business magazine *Forbes*, Matt Damon deserved another kind of recognition. In its annual list of the 100 most

Matt has received many awards for his acting, including the prestigious American Cinematheque Award in 2010. Despite his fame, the talented actor prefers to keep his private life private. As a result, whenever he gives interviews to promote his films, he tends to avoid sharing much personal information.

powerful celebrities of 2007, it called him the movie star who delivered "the best bang for the buck." *Forbes* Celebrity 100 didn't list Matt as the top celebrity. He ranked 52nd. And he didn't make the highest salary per film, either.

But the magazine called Matt "Hollywood's best investment." It noted that his past three films had earned the studios $29 for every $1 they paid him, so *Forbes* considered him to be Hollywood's "most bankable star." Coming in at second place was actor Brad Pitt, who earned the studios only $24 for every $1 of his salary. Motion pictures featuring Matt as a leading actor or supporting costar have grossed a total of approximately $2 billion.

Aging Suburban Dad?

An even more unusual form of recognition would come Matt's way later in 2007. In its November 26 issue, *People Magazine* featured him on its cover, naming him the "Sexiest Man Alive." Matt had initially turned down the title. In a letter that was published in the same issue, he explained that he wasn't the right guy to succeed his buddy George Clooney to the title. But he thanked the editors at *People*, saying:

> "You gave an aging suburban dad the ego boost of a lifetime. My 9-year-old stepdaughter now thinks I'm cool—well, cooler—and although the rest of the world will remain in the dark about this, my wife now knows she's married to almost the sexiest guy alive. And that fact alone may get me out of doing the dishes once in a while."

In addition to publishing the letter in which Matt tried to turn down the award, the editors of *People* noted that the fact he made that attempt justified their choice:

> "[It] perfectly demonstrates many of the reasons we chose him in the first place: irresistible sense of humor, rock-solid family man (he and wife Luciana have two daughters), heart-melting humility."

During his years at Cambridge Rindge and Latin High School, in Cambridge, Massachusetts, Matt Damon was active in theater—as were many of his friends. One of Matt's fellow students who also shared his dream of becoming a film actor was childhood friend Ben Affleck. Both boys knew from an early age that acting would be in their future.

2

A Shared Dream

MATTHEW PAIGE DAMON WAS BORN ON October 8, 1970, in Cambridge, Massachusetts. At the time, his family lived in the nearby town of Newton. His mother, Nancy Carlsson-Paige, was a professor of early childhood development. His father, Kent Damon, worked in the real estate and financial industries. Matt joined an older brother, Kyle, who was three years old.

Matt's parents divorced when he was two years old. Although his father remained close to the family, Matt was raised according to his mother's ideas about child rearing, which included a need for creative play. In December 1997, he told *Interview* magazine:

> "So growing up for me was like you'd get some blocks and then you'd have to go make up a game. I was always making up stories and acting out plays; that's just the way I was raised."

MATT DAMON

Creative play included taking classes at the Wheelock Family Theater, in Boston. Matt knew he wanted to be an actor by the time he was eight.

A Lifelong Friendship

When Matt was ten, Nancy bought a run-down house in Cambridge, Massachusetts, with five other teachers. She moved her boys to the house, which became a six-family co-op. Living in the communal group was a big transition for a 10-year-old. However, the move meant that Matt met another kid who shared his dream of being an actor. Ben Affleck, who was two years younger than Matt, had already worked as a professional actor in television. Their meeting was the start of a lifelong friendship.

> **CROSS-CURRENTS**
> If you would like to learn more about the place where Matt Damon grew up, read "Cambridge." Go to page 47.

Matt got his first professional acting job at age 17, while he was still in high school. He had a single line in the 1988 film *Mystic Pizza*, a romantic comedy that starred newcomers Annabeth Gish, Lilli Taylor, and Julia Roberts. Later that year, he worked as an extra in the drama *The Good Mother*, starring Diane Keaton and Liam Neeson.

Harvard

Matt was serious about acting, but it wasn't the only thing he was good at. His grades at Cambridge Rindge and Latin High School were so high that his principal suggested Matt apply to his hometown college, Harvard. Growing up in Cambridge, Matt had never even considered Harvard. He told an interviewer that because he was a "townie" (a resident of a university town), he thought a school like Harvard would never accept him:

> **"Because I grew up in Central [Square] and we are proprietary about our city—we kind of viewed Harvard students in a different light. I always had an underdog complex growing up."**

To his surprise, Matt was accepted at Harvard, an unusual accomplishment for a Cambridge townie.

A Shared Dream

Matt Damon and Ben Affleck, who is two years younger, had known each other since elementary school. They remained friends in high school, often meeting in the cafeteria for lunchtime discussions about their acting careers. Ben had better luck; during the 1980s he appeared in a television after-school movie special and was a regular on a PBS series.

In the fall of 1988, Matt entered Harvard as a freshman. Officially an English major, he took every drama class he could, studying with nationally acclaimed drama professor David Wheeler of the American Repertory Theater. Matt worked hard and maintained a high grade point average at a school famous for its academic standards. At the same time, he continued to focus on his dream of an acting career and would regularly **audition** for movie roles.

MATT DAMON

In October 1989, Matt was cast in a major role in *Rising Son*, an original television drama for the TNT network. Getting the part was an important break for the aspiring young actor, but it meant Matt had to take a semester off for filming. He took time off from school again to film *School Ties* in the fall of 1991 and *Geronimo:*

Matt took time off from Harvard so he could play a part in *School Ties*, a 1992 film about anti-Semitism in a 1950s-era prep school for boys. The film starred, from left to right, Brendan Fraser, Cole Hauser, and Matt Damon. Matt's good friend Ben Affleck also had a role in the movie.

A Shared Dream

An American Legend in the fall of 1992. When the rest of his class graduated that spring, Matt was almost a year behind.

✦ "Extended Leave" from Harvard ✦

Just 12 credits short of graduation, Matt took a gamble. He took an "extended leave" from Harvard and joined his friend Ben Affleck, who had moved to California to pursue an acting career. Matt moved into Ben's tiny apartment in Eagle Rock, a neighborhood in northeastern Los Angeles.

Competition for film roles was intense. Hundreds of young actors were competing for a handful of parts. Matt and Ben auditioned for roles in films and television, but had little success. Matt did turn down a role in *The Quick and the Dead*, starring Sharon Stone. And he accepted a small part in director Percy Adlon's *Younger and Younger*. Ben had the lead in a bad comedy, *Glory Daze*, and a part in a Burger King commercial.

> **CROSS-CURRENTS**
> To find out more about the life and career of Matt's close friend, check out "Ben Affleck."
> Go to page 48 ▶▶

Frustrated at their inability to get the parts or auditions they wanted, the two unemployed actors began working on a **screenplay** based on a story that Matt had written in a creative writing class at Harvard. They planned on raising about $25,000 and making an independent film in which they could display their skills as actors.

By the end of 1993, the script was more than 1,000 pages long—ten times longer than the average movie script. Not sure what to do with the screenplay, they decided to show it to Matt's talent agent, who turned it over to Patrick Whitesell in the agency's literary department. Whitesell loved the script and suggested that Matt and Ben sell it to a studio instead of trying to make the movie themselves.

On Sunday, November 13, 1994, the script for *Good Will Hunting* was offered for sale to Hollywood's film and television studios in a four-day auction. Matt and Ben watched in amazement as the offers rolled in. The first bid was $15,000; the final offer came in just before the auction closed. Castle Rock Entertainment purchased the script for more than $500,000, with the condition that Matt and Ben play the two lead characters. It looked like their luck had turned.

Searching for stardom in Hollywood in the 1990s, Matt went to numerous auditions. However, most of the roles went to others. His roommates, Ben Affleck and Affleck's younger brother, Casey, were also trying to establish acting careers. Matt and Ben finally decided that they would have to create their own opportunity—by writing the screenplay for *Good Will Hunting*.

3

A Shooting Star

THE RELATIONSHIP WITH CASTLE ROCK ENTER-tainment started out well. Matt and Ben met with actor-director Rob Reiner, one of the partners at the film and television studio. He made several suggestions to improve the script. In the rewrite, Matt and Ben were advised to get rid of certain sections and make the character-driven plot the heart of the story.

By the end of the meeting, most of the unwieldy parts of the script had been discarded. Matt and Ben were left with the basic story about a math **prodigy** who is discovered while working as a janitor at MIT. That storyline was only 63 pages out of the more than 1,000 pages of the original screenplay. For six months, Matt and Ben worked on rewriting the script, turning in draft and after draft but getting no feedback from the studio.

MATT DAMON

⇒ Courage Under Fire ⇐

In the summer of 1995, rewriting came to a halt when Matt got an important role in the film *Courage Under Fire*. The project was the first major Hollywood film about the Persian Gulf War, the 1991 conflict pitting the United States and its allies against Iraq.

Based on a novel by Patrick Sheane Duncan, *Courage Under Fire* tells the story of Captain Karen Emma Walden (played by Meg Ryan), a medevac helicopter pilot who dies during the conflict. Col. Nat Sterling (Denzel Washington) is assigned to investigate Walden's death after she is nominated posthumously

Col. Nat Sterling (Denzel Washington, left) asks questions of Ilario (Matt Damon) in scene from *Courage Under Fire*. To play the character, who becomes a physically ravaged, heroin addict, Damon intentionally lost 40 pounds. "By the end of it, if I stood up, I didn't have any energy," he later told *People* magazine.

for a Congressional Medal of Honor. In the course of his investigation, Sterling uncovers an ugly story of mutiny and betrayal. Matt plays one of her crewmembers, a guilt-ridden medic named Ilario, who is tormented by his memories of the events leading to Walden's death.

With two major stars in the lead roles, *Courage Under Fire* looked like it would be a very high-profile movie, and Matt wanted to make the most of the opportunity. He chose to emphasize the physical effects of guilt on Ilario, who in the years after the war has become a drug addict. In the flashback scenes, shot early in the schedule, Matt is a healthy 180 pounds. But in the later scenes, Matt plays Ilario as a man who is eaten up by guilt. Before filming those scenes, Matt went on a crash diet and lost 41 pounds in three months. He told talk show host Oprah Winfrey how he did it:

> **I ate nothing but egg white and chicken—and I ran 12.8 miles a day every day—and low carbs, one baked potato to two baked potatoes a day.**

Other actors have put on or taken off weight for roles. Robert De Niro put on 60 pounds for the part of the aging Jake LaMotte in *Raging Bull* (1980). Renee Zwelleger put on 30 pounds for *Bridget Jones's Diary* (2001). But those actors made their weight changes under medical supervision. Matt did it on his own. As he told Oprah:

> **I really wasn't a big enough actor for the studio to pay for a nutritionist and I didn't have the money to pay for one, so I was like, well, I'm twenty-five. I'll just do it, and so I did.**

Although Matt was young and healthy, the combination of extreme diet and exercise was dangerous. As a result of abusing his body, Matt had to take medication for the next two years.

➤ TURNAROUND ➤

At the same time that Matt was shooting *Courage Under Fire*, things were coming to a head with *Good Will Hunting*. The deal with Castle Rock that at first had looked like a dream come true had become a nightmare. Unable to reach an agreement with Matt and Ben about

MATT DAMON

what the final script should be, where the film should be shot, or who should direct it, Castle Rock put the script in **turnaround**. This film industry term refers to when a studio sells rights to a project to another studio in exchange for costs of development. Matt and Ben had one month to find another studio to buy out Castle Rock or lose control of the script.

With Castle Rock's development costs added to the original purchase price, the script had doubled in value. But there was little time for either Matt or Ben to sell other studios on the screenplay. Matt was busy working on *Courage Under Fire*. Ben was on the West Coast playing the lead in *Chasing Amy*.

Three days before the deadline, Ben persuaded *Chasing Amy* director Kevin Smith to read the script. The next morning, Smith called Harvey Weinstein, co-chairman of Miramax Pictures. The studio agreed to buy the script from Castle Rock for just under $1 million, the largest amount Miramax had ever paid for an original screenplay.

➤ OUT OF LIMBO ➤

At the beginning of 1996, Matt's career was in limbo. He'd given a brilliant performance in *Courage Under Fire*, but he wasn't getting called for new roles. Miramax had purchased *Good Will Hunting*, but needed to interest a director or a big-name star in the project before it could go anywhere.

Suddenly, everything changed. Matt won the lead role of Rudy Baylor in *The Rainmaker*. Based on a novel by John Grisham, the film was to be directed by Francis Ford Coppola. Matt was now in a position to push for action on *Good Will Hunting*. He told an interviewer:

> ❝The day after I got *The Rainmaker*, I sent Harvey Weinstein a fax. We'd been trying to get *Good Will Hunting* done for a year, and I said 'Dear Harvey, I *am* the Rainmaker, I'm that guy.' He called back and said, 'All right, I'll call you.'❞

CROSS-CURRENTS
If you would like to learn more about the award-winning director of The Rainmaker, read "Francis Ford Coppola." Go to page 49. ➤➤

Soon director Gus Van Sant and **box office** star Robin Williams signed on. The combination of a respected art film director and one of

A Shooting Star

Robin Williams (left) and Matt Damon in a scene from *Good Will Hunting*. Williams first found fame in the 1970s as a comedic actor, but in the mid-1980s he took on dramatic roles as well. In *Good Will Hunting*, he plays a psychologist helping a young math prodigy, played by Matt, come to terms with himself and his abilities.

America's top stars meant the film would attract lots of attention, even with a pair of unknown young actors in two of the lead roles.

⇒ The Role of Private Ryan ⇐

At the same time that Matt was working on *The Rainmaker* and preparing for *Good Will Hunting*, he was pursuing another opportunity. Stephen Spielberg was planning to film a World War II drama in the summer of 1997. Thrilled at the possibility of working with Spielberg but too busy to audition in person, Matt put together an audition tape featuring some of his scenes from *Courage Under Fire*. But Spielberg rejected him.

MATT DAMON

> **CROSS-CURRENTS**
>
> For more information about the director with whom Matt worked on *Saving Private Ryan*, read "Steven Spielberg." Go to page 50. ▶▶

In the course of shooting *Good Will Hunting* in Boston, Matt got a second chance at the part. Spielberg was also in Boston, where he was making the period drama *Amistad*. Robin Williams introduced Matt to Spielberg. It turned out Spielberg had seen Matt only in the audition tape, and had thought the young actor seemed too fragile-looking to play the role. After seeing Matt at his normal weight of 180 pounds, Spielberg hired him for the title role in *Saving Private Ryan*.

▶ SUDDEN CELEBRITY ◀

The Rainmaker opened in theaters in November 1997. The following December, *Good Will Hunting* was released. Reviews for both films were good.

> **CROSS-CURRENTS**
>
> Read "Gus Van Sant" to learn more about the life and career of the director of *Good Will Hunting*. Go to page 51. ▶▶

The back-to-back exposure and the rags-to-riches story of how *Good Will Hunting* came to be made turned Matt into an instant celebrity. That December, he was on the cover of both *Vanity Fair* and *Interview*. He soon appeared on the covers of many other magazines. In January 1998, Matt was interviewed on *The Oprah Winfrey Show*. The same month, he and Ben were invited to the White House for a special screening of *Good Will Hunting* for President and Mrs. Bill Clinton.

Within a year, Matt had gone from being an unemployed actor to working with three critically acclaimed directors. For his performance in *Good Will Hunting*, he was nominated for both the Golden Globe and the **Oscar** for Best Actor. However, it was the screenplay that would bring awards. In January 1998, Matt and Ben Affleck won the Golden Globe for Best Original Screenplay. Two months later, they took home an Oscar.

> **CROSS-CURRENTS**
>
> To learn more about Matt's relationships with costars Clare Danes and Minnie Driver, read "Romance on the Set." Go to page 52. ▶▶

▶ NEW PROJECTS ◀

Matt now had plenty of work. More interested in being an actor than being a star, he chose his new projects carefully, often selecting roles that allowed him to play against type. In a 1998 interview, Matt told a reporter with the *Buffalo News*:

A Shooting Star

At the 70th Academy Awards, held March 23, 1998, Ben Affleck (right) and Matt Damon show off their Oscars for Best Original Screenplay, which they earned for *Good Will Hunting*. Matt was also nominated for Best Actor in the film, which generated more than $137 million at the box office.

MATT DAMON

Matt and his costar Gwyneth Paltrow from *The Talented Mr. Ripley* share a laugh with talk show host Oprah Winfrey (right) during her November 22, 1999, show. Damon and Paltrow were promoting the new film, which tells about a man willing to do anything—even commit murder—in a desperate effort to fit in upper-class society.

> "You start seeing mistakes in careers when people start doing movies and you can see the reasons they're doing it. 'I need to do this big studio movie,' etc. You see people blunder because their heart's not in it. [Tom] Hanks is a really good example [of the right way to do it]. He told me . . . about movies that he passed on, movies that were good movies but that he's really happy he passed on because his heart wasn't in it."

A Shooting Star

In quick succession, Matt played a poker-hustler turned law student in *Rounders* (1998), a fallen angel trying to get back into heaven in *Dogma* (1999), and a charming serial killer in *The Talented Mr. Ripley* (1999). He also made **cameo** appearances in films made by his friends and did **voice-overs** for *Titan A.E* (2000), *The Majestic* (2001), *Spirit: Stallion of the Cimarron* (2002), and *Howard Zinn: You Can't Be Neutral on a Moving Train* (2004).

LivePlanet

In June 2000, Matt teamed up with Ben Affleck to found an entertainment company they called LivePlanet. In addition to other projects, LivePlanet produced an HBO reality series and screenwriting contest named *Project Greenlight*, which first aired in 2001. The show documented aspiring filmmakers' efforts to create a movie. In a 2002 interview with Oprah Winfrey, Matt explained how the show came to be:

> **"Project Greenlight was kind of an answer to a question that Ben and I got after *Good Will Hunting*. Writers would come up to us on the street and say 'What's the best way for me to pursue this?' We didn't really have an answer for them.
>
> So this is our answer, and it was a pretty big idea. It's our belief that there are really talented people out there who deserve a chance. It's just [a matter of] getting the access."**

Matt and Ben produced three of the films developed through *Project Greenlight*: *Stolen Summer* (2002), *The Battle of Shaker Heights* (2003), and *Feast* (2006). None of the movies generated by the program proved financially successful, but *Project Greenlight* was recognized in 2002, 2004, and 2005 with Emmy nominations for Outstanding Reality Program.

A publicity shot from the Western drama *All the Pretty Horses*, which was released in 2000. The film, which also starred Penelope Cruz, was panned by critics and fared poorly at the box office. However, Matt soon followed it up with blockbusters that placed him back on the Hollywood A-List.

Back on the A-List

IN 2000, MATT'S CAREER HIT A SLUMP AFTER HE starred in two movies that failed at the box office. *The Legend of Bagger Vance*, directed by Robert Redford, is the story of a World War I veteran who has lost confidence in himself. The Western drama *All the Pretty Horses* is an adaptation of Cormac McCarthy's prize-winning novel.

There were serious problems with both movies. In *The Legend of Bagger Vance*, a young Matt was cast in a role that was originally intended for Redford, who had been playing romantic leads long before Matt was born. *All the Pretty Horses* suffered from another issue. Many viewers had problems following the film, which had been cut from Billy Bob Thornton's original version of three hours and twelve minutes to less than two hours.

> **CROSS-CURRENTS**
> To learn more about one of the most influential people in Hollywood, read "Robert Redford." Go to page 53. ▶▶

MATT DAMON

Movie careers are fragile things. With back-to-back box office failures, Matt needed a hit to reestablish himself as one of the top actors in the industry—those on Hollywood's A-list. Instead of one hit, he got two.

The Bourne Identity

In 2001, independent director Doug Liman, best known for the 1996 film *Swingers*, asked Matt to play the lead in a film adaptation of Robert Ludlum's spy novel *The Bourne Identity*. In an interview with *Entertainment Weekly*, published in 2002, Matt said that he agreed to do the film in part because of Liman's reputation for directing freewheeling character-driven movies. He explained:

> **[I wanted to] try an action movie . . . exactly the way I'd love to do it, with someone who was thinking out of the box. Doug being Doug, this would be an interesting movie.**

Many Hollywood insiders thought that Matt was an unlikely choice to play an action hero. But Jason Bourne is an unlikely action hero—an assassin for the U.S. Central Intelligence Agency (CIA), who can't remember who he is.

The movie begins with Bourne being dragged out of the ocean with two bullets in his back. Embedded in his hip is a capsule with the number of a Swiss bank account. While searching for clues to his identity, Bourne comes to the attention of his former employers, who send assassins to kill him. Although he has lost his memory, Bourne has not lost his skills. He is forced to fight his way across Europe to escape the killers, even though he doesn't know why they want him dead. In an interview with *Entertainment Weekly*, Matt describes the role:

CROSS-CURRENTS
Check out "Author Robert Ludlum" to find out more about the novelist who created the character of Jason Bourne. Go to page 54.

> **Normally, I've played people searching for who they are. This is the first time I played a guy where, instead of struggling with his identity, he had a real sense of self. Then, well, he forgot it.**

Back on the A-List

Matt prepared for the film with the same seriousness that had led him to lose weight for *Courage Under Fire* and learn to play the piano for *The Talented Mr. Ripley*. Determined to do as many of his own stunts as possible, he worked for six months with a trainer and the film's stunt coordinator, who taught Matt basic stunt work and

Matt made his debut as an action hero in *The Bourne Identity*, which was released in June 2002. Critics raved over his portrayal of Jason Bourne, an assassin with amnesia. The critical and financial success of the film, which took in $27 million during its first weekend, helped Matt Damon become one of the most sought-after actors in Hollywood.

MATT DAMON

Filipino sword and stick fighting. He spent several hundred hours on a shooting range with a former SWAT shot gunner until he could hold a handgun as if it were an extension of his arm. To make himself credible as a trained assassin and to change the way he walked and defined his personal space, he also learned to box.

The shoot was grueling. Liman dragged the *Bourne Identity* cast across Europe, shooting scenes in Prague, Czech Republic; Paris, France; Rome, Italy; Mykonos, Greece; and Zurich, Switzerland. The script, only loosely based on Ludlum's best-selling novel, was in constant rewrite. Matt was exhausted by the stunt work. After deciding that the final scenes of the film just didn't work, Liman brought the cast back to Paris for a reshoot almost a year after production had ended.

When *The Bourne Identity* was finally released in June 2002, it was an unexpected hit. Since then, it has grossed $122 million at the box office, become a bestselling DVD, and transformed Matt's career. When Mark Cina of *US Weekly* asked how the role in *The Bourne Identity* had affected Matt, he said:

> **"It has had the biggest impact on my career. Before I did [*The Bourne Identity*], no one had offered me a movie in six months. After it opened I had 20 offers."**

Ocean's Eleven

Matt followed the gritty tension of *The Bourne Identity* with a role in Steven Soderbergh's remake of the 1960 film *Ocean's Eleven*. With no pretensions of being anything more than a star-studded romp, *Ocean's Eleven* was smart as well as playful, packed with in-jokes on the art of moviemaking. The film starred George Clooney as Danny Ocean, a paroled ex-con out to rob three of the most popular casinos in Las Vegas. In order to pull off the heist, he puts together an all-star team of criminal specialists.

Matt plays Linus Caldwell, a small-time pickpocket who is serving his apprenticeship as a big-time thief. The role is very different from that of Jason Bourne. The Bourne character is tough, experienced, and driven. Linus is naïve and untested. The rest of Ocean's eleven-man team give him all the dirty jobs and regularly have fun at his expense.

Back on the A-List

Ocean's Eleven was shot after *The Bourne Identity*, although it was released in December 2001, well before Matt won acclaim as Jason Bourne. Stephen Soderbergh directed the comic caper, which made more than $183 million during its five-month run in theaters. Its stars included (from left to right) George Clooney, Brad Pitt, Matt Damon, Elliott Gould, and Don Cheadle.

Taking Artistic Chances

The success of *The Bourne Identity* allowed Matt to choose the roles he wanted to play without regard to their commercial potential. Like actors Robin Williams and Tom Hanks before him, Matt accepted a role because he liked the project, he liked the director, or just because he wanted to try something new.

Together with Casey Affleck, Ben's younger brother, Matt wrote and starred in Gus van Sant's film, *Gerry* (2002). It is an experimental film about two men named Gerry who are stranded in the desert and must struggle for survival. Although film buffs praised the movie for its beautiful camerawork, most American audiences found it too far from the **mainstream** to enjoy.

MATT DAMON

Matt also took some television roles. He displayed a previously unseen gift for comedy in an episode of the TV show *Will and Grace*, in which he played a straight man pretending to be gay so he can sing in a gay chorus. Afterward, directors Peter and Bobby Farrelly, best known for *Something about Mary*, offered Matt a role as the shy half of a pair of Siamese twins in the comedy film *Stuck on You* (2003). The movie was typical of the Farrelly brothers' work, combining broad **slapstick** humor with sentimentality. Reviews ranged from raves to groans.

In 2005, Matt appeared as Bavarian fairytale collector Wilhelm Grimm in Terry Gilliam's fantasy *The Brothers Grimm* and as an oil

In the 2005 fantasy film *The Brothers Grimm*, Matt Damon and Heath Ledger costarred as traveling con artists in 19th-century Germany who encounter a real-life fairytale curse. Although the movie was praised for its beautiful imagery, its story did not satisfy most critics and most moviegoers were not at all enchanted.

Back on the A-List

analyst working in the Middle East in the geopolitical thriller *Syriana*. Reviewers found *The Brothers Grimm* dull and incoherent and *Syriana* too complicated.

In a July 2004 interview, *Entertainment Weekly* asked Matt to explain his choices in film roles. He insisted he has no regrets about the projects he's worked on. He replied:

> **"I'd go back and make the same choices. When these movies don't work, it's not for lack of trying. You're taking a big swing, and if it doesn't work out, it doesn't work out on a big scale."**

Commercial Security

Matt returned to the roles of **amnesiac** assassin Jason Bourne and pickpocket Linus Caldwell in 2004. In the **sequel** to *The Bourne Identity*, called *The Bourne Supremacy*, documentary filmmaker Paul Greengrass replaced Doug Liman as the director. Known for fast-paced, naturalistic filmmaking, Greengrass retained the balance between spy thriller and character study that Liman had brought to the original film. Dubbed a thinking man's action film, the sequel was an even bigger financial success than the first Bourne movie, grossing $53 million on its opening weekend.

The same year, Matt appeared in another sequel, this one a follow-up to *Ocean's Eleven*. In *Ocean's Twelve*, Danny Ocean's crew was back in action, in a race with a notorious cat burglar to steal a jewel-studded Faberge egg from a museum in Rome.

Matt's character, Linus, has a bigger part of the action in the sequel. Still naïve and the butt of the group's jokes, he nonetheless takes charge of the heist when Interpol throws Danny into jail. (Danny's arrest is in its own way a joke on Linus, who doesn't know the arrest is part of the group's plan to steal the jeweled egg.)

The film was a financial success. However, many critics agreed that the sequel lacked the sparkle of the first film.

Matt Gets Married

While filming the comedy *Stuck on You* in Miami Beach, Florida, in 2003, Matt met bartender and single mom Luciana Bozan Barroso. After dating for a couple of years, they were married in December 2005. During the early years of their marriage, Matt and Luciana

MATT DAMON

Matt and his wife Luciana attend the premiere of his 2009 film *Invictus*. The two were quietly married in New York on December 9, 2005. Matt became a stepdad to Alexia, Luciana's seven-year-old daughter from a previous marriage. They have three other daughters together.

chose to live a quiet life in Miami, so that Luciana's daughter from a first marriage, Alexia, could be close to her father. By 2010, however, the family had moved to Manhattan, where they currently live with Alexia and their three younger children: Isabella (born 2006), Gia (born 2008) and Stella (born 2010).

In an interview with World Entertainment News Network, Matt attributed his family's ability to avoid the **paparazzi** to the fact that Luciana is not a celebrity:

> "I'm with a normal girl and it's great. People don't know who she is, don't care that I'm with her and never follow us around. There's a lesson—if you like a low-profile life away from filming, then don't date another celebrity. This is what I've always wanted. I can do the acting, live my life, enjoy the attention and not be chased because I'm with someone well-known."

Many superstars have to fight off reporters anytime they step outside their house. Matt can go out with his wife and children without being hassled.

Matt decided early on in his career to try to avoid most of the hype of stardom. Years ago, he told the *Calgary Sun* that he had watched how rock stars Michael Jackson and Bruce Springsteen handled fame in the mid-1980s. Jackson would travel with more than 20 bodyguards, while Springsteen preferred to go off on his own. Damon said then that he'd rather be like Bruce Springsteen, stating:

> "Fame is what you make of it. I'm never going to do the whole bodyguard nonsense. It's just not me. . . . I never considered myself guarded [before], so I'd talk about my personal life. I can't do that any more and that's unfortunate. That's one lesson I've learned about fame."

Matt Damon chats with director Martin Scorsese (front, left) during filming of the 2006 crime drama *The Departed*. The story centers on two undercover agents—Matt Damon as a mob member who joins the police force and Leonardo DiCaprio as a police mole working for the mob. *Entertainment Weekly* called Damon's performance "career-defining."

5
New Roles

OVER THE COURSE OF FOUR YEARS, MATT HAD made eight movies, ranging from *The Bourne Identity* to *Ocean's Twelve*. He joked that the only thing that would stop him from taking time off from work would be a call saying director Martin Scorsese wanted to use him in a film. He soon had that opportunity.

The Departed

At the beginning of 2006, Matt was back in Boston and working on a new film that was being directed by Martin Scorsese. Most moviegoers consider Scorsese to be one of the most important filmmakers of his generation. Over the course of three decades, he has consistently directed powerful movies, beginning in 1973 with his first major film, *The Mean Streets* (1973).

Although Scorsese is best known for the movies in which he directed Robert De Niro, including *Taxi Driver* (1976), *Raging Bull* (1980), and *Goodfellas* (1990), his work has never been limited to themes of urban violence. He has directed films as different as *Alice Doesn't Live Here Any More* (1974), the lavish musical *New York, New York* (1977), the concert film *The Last Waltz* (1978), and the controversial *The Last Temptation of Christ* (1988). Though Scorsese has never won an Academy Award himself, many actors have been nominated for their work under his direction.

In early 2006, Matt had the opportunity to work with Scorsese in filming *The Departed*, which also starred Jack Nicholson, Leonardo DiCaprio, and Mark Wahlberg. Matt took on the role of Colin Sullivan, a street-smart criminal who infiltrates the Massachusetts State Police so that he can feed information to powerful crime boss Frank Costello (Nicholson). DiCaprio played his police counterpart, a cop who is working undercover in Costello's Boston crime gang. Unlike DiCaprio, Boston-born Matt didn't have to work to master South Boston's distinctive accent. He spent his preparation time riding along with members of the Massachusetts State Police, learning to make his performance as a double agent in the police force more authentic. He even went with the police when they raided a crack house.

The training as a police officer had limits, however. Matt told a reporter for *The Harvard Crimson*:

> **"You remember that movie 'The Hard Way', with Michael J. Fox? I was kind of like Fox, like 'Hey guys, can I have a gun?' And they were like, 'Shut up, no.' They didn't give me a gun, luckily for all of us."**

THE GOOD SHEPHERD

Matt hardly had time to catch his breath before beginning work later that year on Robert De Niro's *The Good Shepherd*. Although De Niro had directed only one other film, his reputation as an actor was so impressive that few actors would turn down the chance to work with him. De Niro is best known for his work with Martin Scorsese and his role as the young Vito Corleone in *The Godfather, Part II* (1974).

In *The Good Shepherd*, Matt plays another character who works undercover—CIA agent Edward Wilson. Based on the life of longtime CIA Chief of Counter-Intelligence James J. Angleton, *The Good Shepherd* traces the history of the intelligence agency through Wilson's career. The story begins in the early 1940s, when Wilson is

New Roles

Angelina Jolie plays Matt Damon's long-suffering wife in the espionage thriller *The Good Shepherd*, directed by Robert De Niro, and released in 2006. An account of the early years of the CIA is woven in with the fictional story of an agent, played by Matt, who becomes emotionally detached from others as he rises to power in the firm.

a Yale graduate who is recruited to gather intelligence for the Office of Strategic Services during World War II. He stays in the agency when the wartime OSS evolves into the CIA, and through the years becomes an emotionless man who makes choices that eventually contradict the ideals he held when he first joined the service.

In December 2006, Matt told *USA Today* that the shoot for *The Good Shepherd* was the most exhausting he had ever done, even when compared to the physically demanding stunts required in the *Bourne* films:

MATT DAMON

> "It was a hard movie. [De Niro] had been thinking about it for years. You'd do take after take. His attention to detail is unbelievable. His drive to do this movie was intense. Every day was 16 or 18 hours. No exaggeration."

FATHERHOOD

After a year of challenging roles in 2006, Matt returned to the familiar ground of sequels in *Ocean's Thirteen* and *The Bourne Ultimatum*. Both were released in 2007. Once again, Danny Ocean's crew had a great time on the set. Once again, Jason Bourne raced to uncover the mystery of his past. Once again, both sequels were big hits.

A scene from the 2007 film *Ocean's Thirteen*. In May and June 2007 actors in the glitzy movie—George Clooney, Brad Pitt, Matt Damon, and Don Cheadle—organized several benefits around the film's premiere to raise funds to help the people of Darfur, a war-torn region of Sudan.

New Roles

However, Matt's took on a whole new role in 2006 when he became a father. On June 11, he and wife Luciana welcomed the birth their daughter Isabella. Six months later, the new dad had nothing but good things to say about being a father. In a press conference held to launch *The Good Shepherd*, he was asked to describe what it was like to be a dad. He replied:

> **"It's great, great. That's been just amazing. It defies description, actually. I don't really know how to talk about it because I don't really know—I feel like I got made a member of a club that I didn't know existed."**

At one interview, Matt even went so far as to claim that his sleepless nights with baby Isabella contributed to his characterization of Jason Bourne in *The Bourne Ultimatum*. Getting inadequate amounts of sleep gave him a look of exhaustion that he couldn't have produced on his own.

With the birth of Isabella, Matt began to think about using the power of celebrity to make a difference in the world. In December, 2006, he told *InStyle*:

> **"Having a kid changes you. It forces you to move outside yourself and start thinking about what the world is going to look like after you're gone."**

⇒ Changing the World ⇐

The desire to help others has led Matt to use his celebrity to bring attention to the extreme poverty in Africa. Matt has become involved with DATA (Debt AIDS Trade Africa), an organization founded by rock star Bono and other activists to raise awareness of issues in Africa. Matt has also worked with ONE: The Campaign to Make Poverty History. ONE is a nonprofit organization that works to eliminate extreme poverty and AIDS in Africa.

In May 2006, Matt traveled with ONE on a six-day listening and learning trip to Zambia, in southern Africa. He described the impact of that visit in a letter posted on the ONE Web site:

CROSS-CURRENTS
If you would like to learn more about Matt's charitable work, check out "Matt Damon's Causes." Go to page 54. ▶

MATT DAMON

> "To see so much hope from people who have so little made this an inspiring and life changing journey for me. The promises America and other rich countries have made to Africa must be more than words. Those promises need to put hopeful children in school; help parents put roofs over the heads of their children; and get lifesaving AIDS medicines to the patients who need them now."

While he was in Zambia, Matt saw how little it takes to make a difference between defeat and survival. He visited a credit program that loans very small amounts of money to people to start home-based businesses. He also stopped at an organic cotton farm and a clinic that treats AIDS victims. At the AIDS clinic, Matt made a video celebrating the courage of people living with the disease.

His trip to Africa made Matt aware of the serious water problems that people on the continent face each day. He described the experience:

> "My friends at the ONE Campaign and DATA brought me to Zambia and South Africa, where I witnessed extreme poverty and the role that clean drinking water plays in getting millions out of danger. I learned that a child dies every 15 seconds due to diseases from dirty water."

When Matt came home, he wanted to do something to help. He decided to get involved with a project that a friend told him about: Three men were planning to run 4,500 miles across the Sahara Desert to bring attention to the water crisis in Africa. The project was called the Running the Sahara expedition. Soon, Matt had his production company, LivePlanet, involved with filming the event. LivePlanet has helped produce and Matt narrates the resulting documentary, called *Running the Sahara*.

Matt and others founded a group called H2O Africa, a clean water initiative designed to build on the publicity generated by the Running the Sahara expedition. LivePlanet also created a television program called *Beyond the Expedition: Running the Sahara*, which was released in late 2007.

New Roles

> As a matter of fact, the water you drink does make a difference.
>
> — Matt Damon

Over one billion people around the world lack clean water. Join me in my partnership with Ethos Water and H2O Africa and make a difference in the world water crisis. Every time you buy a bottle of Ethos, money goes to help provide children with the access to clean water they need. So if you choose to drink bottled water, please choose to make a difference. To learn more, visit ethoswater.com.

Every Bottle Makes a Difference.™

Ethos is a proud supporter of "Running The Sahara." In theaters this spring.

A donation of $0.05 is made for every bottle of Ethos sold toward the Ethos Water Fund goal of donating $10 million by 2010.

Matt Damon has been involved in programs intended to bring clean drinking water to people in poor or underdeveloped African countries. In 2006 he founded H2O Africa, a non-governmental organization (NGO) that provides aid to regions that do not have safe drinking water or sanitation. The organization has funded projects in Uganda, Mauritania, Mali, and the Central African Republic.

MATT DAMON

Matt Damon attends a 2011 movie premiere. Thanks to the great financial success of his past films, the talented actor is free to choose roles that interest him.

> **CROSS-CURRENTS**
> To learn how Matt has worked to help the people of war-torn Sudan, read "Not on Our Watch." Go to page 55.

In addition to his work with ONE and H2O Africa, Matt along with George Clooney, Brad Pitt, Don Cheadle, and Jerry Weintraub founded the Not on Our Watch Project, a fund-raising and advocacy group that works to help victims of genocide and other atrocities. At home, Matt is a spokesperson for Feeding America, a group that runs more than 200 food banks in the United States. He is also on the board of Tonic Mailstopper, an organization devoted to reducing the environmental impact of junk mail by cutting down the amount of junk mail its members receive and by planting one tree every month for each member.

New Roles

What's Next?

Matt Damon remains one of Hollywood's most marketable stars. In recent years he's starred in such films as *The Informant* (2009), directed by his friend Stephen Soderbergh, the 2010 remake of *True Grit*, and the 2011 romantic comedy *We Bought a Zoo*.

With an impressive body of work already behind him, Matt is looking forward to a long career. The financial success of the *Bourne* trilogy and other films has given him the freedom to make bold choices about future roles. As he explained to an interviewer from *US Weekly*:

> "The careers I look at are George Clooney's and Clint Eastwood's. They're doing it on their own terms. I'd love to have a long career, but it's hard in this business. I'm still here . . . and I think we're all amazed by that!"

Matt may be the only one who is amazed. In that same interview, director Stephen Soderbergh, who worked with Matt on *Ocean's Eleven* and several other films, said:

> "Anybody who has worked with [Matt] respects him and knows he's a terrific actor. He's going to put together a pretty significant body of work. He's just going to get better as he gets older."

CROSS-CURRENTS

Grauman's Chinese Theater

Grauman's Chinese Theatre was one of several elaborate movie palaces that were built across the United States between 1910 and 1929. Designed to look like a traditional Chinese pagoda, or Buddhist temple, the theater opened in 1927 for the premiere of Cecil B. DeMille's new epic *The King of Kings*. Thousands of fans rioted on Hollywood Boulevard, trying to get a glimpse of movie stars and other celebrities as they arrived. Today fans still line up outside the Chinese Theatre to see the stars arrive for movie premieres.

Grauman's Chinese Theater is best known for its courtyard, where since 1927 Hollywood legends have left their signatures and footprints in cement blocks. The tradition began by accident, when showman Sid Grauman stepped in wet cement in the courtyard a few days before the theater opened. The first star to leave her footprints in the courtyard was silent film idol Mary Pickford.

Not every star left a footprint. Groucho Marx made an impression of his cigar. Roy Rogers marked his cement block with an imprint of his gun, next to the hoof prints of his horse, Trigger. Jimmy Durante buried his famous nose in wet cement. Daniel Radcliffe, Emma Watson, and Rupert Grint, stars of the Harry Potter movies, left impressions of their wands.

The Grauman's Chinese Theater is a Hollywood landmark in Los Angeles, California. Since its opening in May 1927, the theater has been visited by millions of people. Some flock to the landmark to glimpse famous stars at movie premiers. Others visit the courtyard to look at the handprints, footprints, and other impressions left in concrete by various entertainers.

(Go back to page 7.) ◀◀

CROSS-CURRENTS

Cambridge

Matt grew up in Cambridge, Massachusetts—a city with a long history. First settled by English Puritans in 1630, Cambridge became an important industrial center in the early 19th century in part because of its proximity to the growing city of Boston. Cambridge attracted various industries, particularly furniture, glass, and brick-making factories. Immigrants eager for jobs flocked to the town and the population grew rapidly. Many were emigrants from Ireland, who were fleeing the potato famine of 1845. By 1855, Irish immigrants made up 22 percent of the city's population. The Irish were followed by Italians, Poles, Portuguese, Germans, French Canadians, and Russian Jews.

In the early 1900s, the industrial base of the city began to decline. Instead of factories, universities became major employers in Cambridge. The city is the home of two prestigious U.S. universities: Harvard University and the Massachusetts Institute of Technology (MIT). More recently, cutting edge companies in information technologies and biotechnology have established offices in Cambridge.

The city's population includes a diverse mixture of students and professors from Harvard and MIT, working class families, and immigrants. Students from 82 different countries attend its public schools.

(Go back to page 12.) ⏪

A view across the Charles River, with the city of Cambridge in the background. Matt Damon and Ben Affleck grew up in Cambridge in houses just two blocks away from each other. Some favorite hangouts of the two friends included Dana Park, where they played basketball, and the movie theaters at Harvard Square.

CROSS-CURRENTS

Ben Affleck

Ben Affleck was born in Berkeley, California in 1972, but grew up in Cambridge, Massachusetts. He worked as a child actor, appearing in several made-for-television movies. At age 12, he landed a role on the educational television series *Voyage of the Mimi*. After graduating from Cambridge Rindge and Latin High School in 1990, Ben attended college briefly but then moved to the West Coast. There, he struggled to build an acting career.

Ben landed a supporting role in the 1992 film *School Ties*, as well as parts in several well-regarded independent films, including *Dazed and Confused* (1993), *Mallrats* (1995), and *Chasing Amy* (1997). But his breakthrough came with *Good Will Hunting* (1997), which he cowrote with lifelong friend Matt Damon. In the film, he played Chuckie, the best friend of the title character.

Ben began to get roles in major films. He had a supporting role in *Shakespeare in Love* (1998) and leads in big budget action films such as *Armageddon* (1998) and *Pearl Harbor* (2001). After a run of box office flops in 2003 and 2004, Ben appeared in 2006 in the critically acclaimed *Hollywoodland*. That same year he wrote and directed *Gone Baby Gone*. The movie opened to rave reviews and led critics to wonder whether Affleck might be better behind the camera than in front of it. (Go back to page 15.) ⏪

Matt's buddy Ben Affleck has had an up-and-down career as an actor. He has starred in box office hits such as The Sum of All Fears *(2002) and* Daredevil *(2003). But he has also appeared in critically panned box office losers, like* Gigli *(2003). His directorial debut—*Gone Baby Gone *(2007)—received much critical acclaim.*

CROSS-CURRENTS

Francis Ford Coppola

Francis Ford Coppola during the filming of Youth Without Youth, *in 2006. Coppola is most renowned for directing the highly regarded Godfather trilogy and the Vietnam War epic* Apocalypse Now. *Damon has a cameo appearance in Coppola's dramatic thriller* Youth Without Youth, *which was the first film Coppola directed since* The Rainmaker *(1997).*

Director and screenwriter Francis Ford Coppola was the first major American filmmaker to emerge from a university filmmaking program. He got his master of fine arts from the University of California, Los Angeles, Film School in 1966.

Coppola came to the attention of Hollywood with two back-to-back successes in the early 1970s. In 1971, he and Edmund North wrote the screenplay for *Patton*, starring George C. Scott, and won the Oscar for Best Original Screenplay. The following year Coppola made a name for himself as director of *The Godfather*.

In the years since *The Godfather*, Coppola has consistently taken artistic chances, pushing the limits of **cinematic** form in almost every film he makes. As a result, his directing career has alternated between creative failures and spectacular hits. His *Godfather* trilogy is considered by many critics to be a major cinematic achievement. Films like *Apocalypse Now* (1979), *The Cotton Club* (1984), and *Tucker* (1988), whatever their artistic merits, failed at the box office and pushed Coppola's American Zoetrope Studio into bankruptcy. More commercial films, like the time-travel comedy *Peggy Sue Got Married* (1986), *Bram Stoker's Dracula* (1992) and *The Rainmaker* (1997), kept Coppola in the game.

(Go back to page 20.)

Steven Spielberg

Director and producer Steven Spielberg is the most commercially successful filmmaker in Hollywood history. He first wowed audiences in the summer of 1975 with the release of his first film, the shark thriller *Jaws*. It was followed by a string of hits, including *Close Encounters of the Third Kind* (1977), *Raiders of the Lost Ark* (1981), and *ET: The Extraterrestrial* (1982). In the mid-1980s, Spielberg had the clout to take on more serious projects, beginning with *The Color Purple* in 1985.

In 1993, Spielberg released two films that epitomized his balancing act between blockbuster hits and more artistically ambitious projects. *Jurassic Park*, a thriller about dinosaurs cloned from prehistoric insects, is a marvel of special effects and one of the highest-grossing films of all time. Many critics consider *Schindler's List*, the story of one man's successful efforts to save Jews during the Holocaust, a masterpiece. It won Oscars for best film and best director.

In 1994, Spielberg founded the production company DreamWorks Studio and worked behind the scenes as an executive producer. He returned to the director's chair in 1997 with *Lost World*, *Amistad*, and *Saving Private Ryan*. Since 1997, he has continued to release both blockbusters and serious dramas.

(Go back to page 22.) ◀◀

On August 11, 1999, director Steven Spielberg (right) received the Department of Defense Medal for Distinguished Public Service in recognition of his film Saving Private Ryan. *The award, presented by Defense Secretary William S. Cohen (left), recognized the film for sparking national awareness of the sacrifices made by the American men and women during World War II.*

CROSS-CURRENTS

Gus Van Sant

Director Gus Van Sant made his reputation with independent films like *Mala Noche* (1985), *Drugstore Cowboy* (1989), and *My Own Private Idaho* (1991). His first films focused on people on the fringes of society. With the release of *To Die For* (1995), featuring Nicole Kidman as a psychopathic weather girl obsessed with stardom, Van Sant turned his sharp eye for human weaknesses on middle-class America.

Good Will Hunting was Van Sant's first mainstream film. His preference for making films about isolated outsiders made him the perfect choice to direct the story of a troubled blue-collar prodigy struggling to find his place in the world. His direction provided edginess to the film that kept the story from becoming too sentimental.

In the years following the release of *Good Will Hunting*, Van Sant returned to more experimental—and less financially successful—films. They have included *Finding Forrester* (2000), a film about the relationship between a Bronx high school student and a reclusive writer, and *Gerry* (2002), a largely **improvised** film about two men stranded in the desert.

Van Sant created an unlikely success in the controversial *Elephant*, a fictional film inspired by the 1999 massacre at Columbine High School. Despite its troubling subject, *Elephant* won the Palm d'Or at the 1993 Cannes Film Festival.

Before he tackled Good Will Hunting, *Gus Van Sant was known for films such as* My Own Private Idaho *(1991) and his adaptation of the Tom Robbins' novel* Even Cowgirls Get the Blues *(1993), both of which starred Keanu Reeves. The famed director is also a photographer, musician, and author.*

(Go back to page 22.) ◀◀

CROSS-CURRENTS

Romance on the Set

Real life sparks between the romantic leads in a movie is one of the clichés of Hollywood life. Early in his career, Matt Damon was involved in two "on the set romances."

Clare Danes played the love interest in *The Rainmaker*, which was shot in late 1996. Although only 17 at the time, she was already a successful television and movie actress. The romance between Matt and Clare filled the gossip pages, but it was only a fling. It ended as soon as the seven weeks of shooting *The Rainmaker* ended.

Matt's relationship with English actress and singer-songwriter Minnie Driver, his romantic interest in *Good Will Hunting*, began during filming in the summer of 1997. When Matt was in England working on *Saving Private Ryan*, he visited her on the set of her movie, *The Governess*. However, in early February 1998, Matt casually announced the end of the relationship during an interview on *The Oprah Winfrey Show*. Viewers assumed that Matt had dumped Minnie on television, and he was attacked in the press for his lack of sensitivity. After that, Matt became more careful about discussing his personal life in interviews.

Matt Damon and Minnie Driver at the Los Angeles premiere of Good Will Hunting, *December 2, 1997. Their relationship did not last a year, but Matt got plenty of bad press when he was falsely accused of breaking up with her on* The Oprah Winfrey Show, *instead of doing so in person.*

Matt dated several other actresses before he met his wife, Luciana Bozan Barroso, in 2003. However, he never again dated his leading lady.

(Go back to page 22.)

CROSS-CURRENTS

Robert Redford

After several years of working on Broadway and making guest appearances on popular television shows, Robert Redford made his film debut in a low-budget movie called *War Hunt* in 1962. He had his big breakthrough in 1969, when he costarred with Paul Newman in *Butch Cassidy and the Sundance Kid*, which was both a critical and a financial hit. *Butch Cassidy* was followed by a string of hits between 1972 and 1977 that made the most of Redford's combination of extraordinary good looks and intelligent acting. Among the biggest hits were *The Sting* (1973), *The Way We Were* (1973), and *All the President's Men* (1976).

In 1980, Redford made the move from actor to director with *Ordinary People*. That film won him his first Oscars, for both Best Film and Best Director. Following the success of *Ordinary People*, Redford's career has swung between acting and directing.

In addition to making films himself, Redford is a champion of independent filmmaking. In 1981, Redford established the Sundance Institute for Young Filmmakers and the Sundance Film Festival. The latter, which began as a showcase for independent films, has become one of the most popular events in the motion picture industry.

(Go back to page 27.) ◀◀

Robert Redford has worked as an actor, director, and producer. He is also well known for establishing an international institute for the arts, in Sundance, Utah, where annual independent film festivals promote works by independent and innovative filmmakers. In 2002 Redford received a special honorary Oscar in recognition of his accomplishments over the years.

CROSS-CURRENTS

Author Robert Ludlum

Actor-turned-novelist Robert Ludlum may be best known for the Bourne trilogy. But in the course of his 30-year writing career, he authored 21 suspense novels, beginning with The Scarlatti Inheritance, in 1971. Published in 32 languages, Ludlum's books were international best sellers. Several of his novels were made into movies or television mini-series. One of them was The Bourne Identity, which in 1988 was adapted as a television mini-series starring Richard Chamberlain and Jaclyn Smith. Ludlum also published under two **pseudonyms**: Jonathan Ryder and Michael Shephard.

Ludlum's novels featured fast-paced plots in which lone heroes fight against global corporations or shadowy government agencies. Carefully researched, his works were notable for accuracy in technical details, such as his descriptions in the Bourne novels of the treatment of **amnesia**.

Ludlum had written only three Bourne thrillers before he died in 2001. Following the success of the movie version of The Bourne Identity, the Ludlum estate gave writer Eric van Lustbader permission to continue the Bourne series. To date, van Lustbader has produced 10 additions to the Bourne saga. The most recent book, The Bourne Imperative, was published in the summer of 2012.

(Go back to page 28.) ◀◀

Matt Damon's Causes

Since the early 2000s, Matt has been actively involved in programs to help make life better for people living in poverty.

A Historic First

The motto of the ONE Campaign is "The Campaign to Make Poverty History." Founded in 2004 by a coalition of 11 humanitarian organizations, ONE has grown to include 2.4 million members. Today, the campaign is made up of more than 100 organizations that deal with the four major issues affecting the lives of children—health, education, clean water, and food.

ONE's primary purpose is to raise public awareness about extreme poverty and the spread of AIDS in the world's poorest countries. A successful method of raising awareness has been to enlist celebrities who are filmed while touring poverty-stricken areas. The resulting videos are then posted on the Internet.

H2O Africa Foundation

H2O Africa is an organization that finances sanitation and clean water projects in Africa. Since 2006, H2O Africa has raised money to support sustainable clean water programs in the Central African Republic, Ethiopia, Niger, Rwanda, and Uganda. Projects include training so facilities can be maintained over time. They are designed to work with other programs. One example of this is a water purification system for a school accompanied by a program that encourages parents to see that their children get to school.

(Go back to page 41.) ◀◀

CROSS-CURRENTS

Not on Our Watch

Not on Our Watch was founded by actors George Clooney, Brad Pitt, Matt Damon, and Don Cheadle, as well as producer Jerry Weintraub. The charity works to bring attention to and provide resources for victims of genocide and other mass atrocities around the world. Instead of creating new relief programs, the organization works through already established aid groups.

One of Not on Our Watch's projects is helping suffering refugees in the Darfur region of the Sudan, where more than 2 million people were driven from their homes as a result of ongoing violence between the Sudanese government and rebel militias. In June 2007, as part of its fundraising activities, Not on Our Watch donated $2.75 million raised at benefit screenings of *Ocean's Thirteen* to the International Relief Committee (IRC) to support aid programs in Darfur.

In 2008, Not on Our Watch contributed another $3.25 million to establish programs in Darfur and the neighboring state of Chad with the help of the IRC, Oxfam America, Save the Children, and the United Nations World Food Program. The organization focuses on providing clean water and basic healthcare to refugee camps, empowering women, who are often the target of violence, and ensuring that vital supplies are delivered safely.

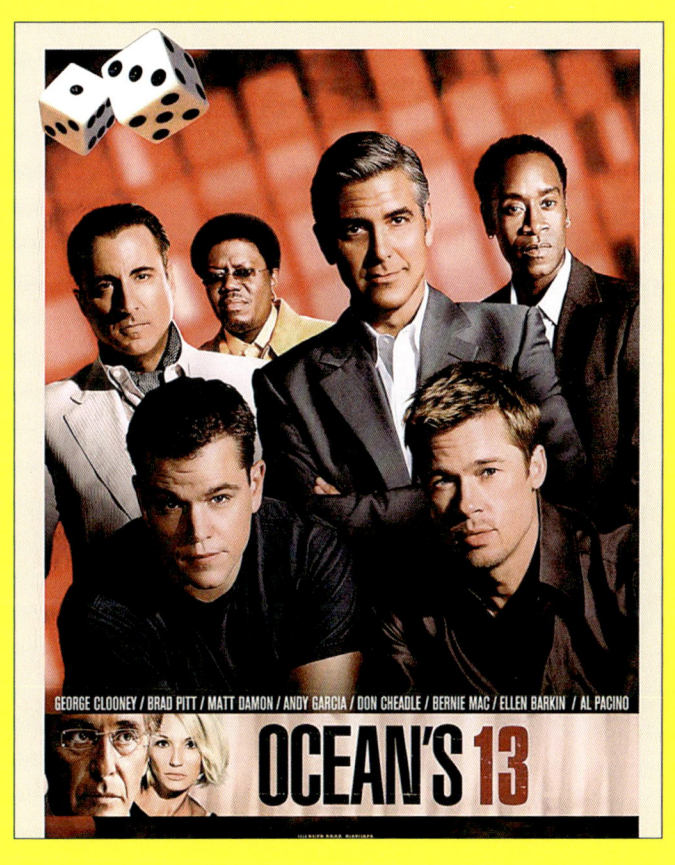

A promotional poster for Ocean's 13. *In the spring of 2007, George Clooney, Matt Damon, Brad Pitt, and Don Cheadle were joined by producer Jerry Weintraub in cofounding Not on Our Watch. The organization was established to help people affected by the genocide occurring in Darfur, Sudan. The millions of dollars raised by the group helps support humanitarian and relief groups working in the region.*

(Go back to page 44.)

CHRONOLOGY

1970 Matthew Paige Damon is born on October 8 in Cambridge, Massachusetts. His parents, Nancy and Kent Damon, bring him home to the village of Newton Corner.

1973 Matt's parents are divorced and his mother assumes the last name of Carlsson-Paige.

1980 Matt's mother moves her two sons, Matt and Kyle, to Cambridge.

1981 Ten-year-old Matt makes friends with eight-year-old Ben Affleck.

1988 Matt lands his first movie role, in the film *Mystic Pizza*.

1989 Matt is cast in a major role in Rising Son (1990), an original drama for the cable television network TNT.

1994 Castle Rock Entertainment buys the script for *Good Will Hunting* for more than $500,000, with the stipulation that writers Matt and Ben play the two main characters.

1995 To look the part for his role in *Courage Under Fire*, Matt loses more than 40 pounds. Miramax Studios purchases the script for *Good Will Hunting* from Castle Rock.

1996 Matt lands his first leading role, playing an embattled young attorney in Francis Ford Coppola's film *The Rainmaker*.

1997 After *The Rainmaker* is released in November and *Good Will Hunting* premieres in December, Matt becomes a media darling. Stephen Spielberg hires Matt for the title role of *Saving Private Ryan*.

1998 In March, Matt and Ben receive the Oscar for Best Original Screenplay for *Good Will Hunting*.

2000 Matt founds LivePlanet with Ben Affleck and sponsors a reality television film competition called *Project Greenlight*.

2002 Matt plays the lead role of Jason Bourne in *The Bourne Identity*.

2005 On December 9, Matt marries Luciana Bozan Barroso.

2006 Matt's first child, Isabella Damon, is born on June 11.

2007 Receives star on the Hollywood Walk of Fame

2009 Nominated for an Oscar for *Invictus*.

2011 *We Bought a Zoo* is a critical and commercial success.

2012 Stars in *Promised Land*, directed by Gus Van Sant.

ACCOMPLISHMENTS & AWARDS

Filmography

1988 *The Good Mother* (uncredited)
Mystic Pizza

1990 *Rising Son*

1992 *School Ties*

1993 *Geronimo: An American Legend*

1995 *The Good Old Boys*

1996 *Courage Under Fire*
Glory Daze (cameo)

1997 *Chasing Amy* (cameo)
Good Will Hunting
The Rainmaker

1998 *Dogma*
Rounders
Saving Private Ryan

1999 *Planet Ice* (voice)
The Talented Mr. Ripley

2000 *All the Pretty Horses*
Finding Forrester
The Legend of Bagger Vance
Titan A.E. (voice)

2001 *Jay and Silent Bob Strike Back* (cameo)
The Majestic (voice)
Ocean's Eleven

2002 *The Bourne Identity*
Confessions of a Dangerous Mind (cameo)
Gerry
Spirit: Stallion of the Cimarron (voice)

2003 *Stuck on You*

2004 *The Bourne Supremacy*
Eurotrip (cameo)
Howard Zinn: You Can't Be Neutral on a Moving Train (voice)
Jersey Girl (cameo)
Ocean's Twelve

ACCOMPLISHMENTS & AWARDS

2005 The Brothers Grimm
         Syriana

2006 The Departed
         The Good Shepherd

2007 The Bourne Ultimatum
         Ocean's Thirteen

2008 Running the Sahara

2009 Invictus
         Green Zone
         The Informant

2010 Hereafter
         True Grit

2011 The Adjustment Bureau
         Contagion
         Margaret
         We Bought a Zoo

2012 Promised Land

Awards

Academy Award, Best Original Screenplay, 1997

Golden Globe, Best Screenplay, 1997

ShoWest Star of Tomorrow, 1998

ShoWest Man of the Year, 2005

American Cinematheque Award, 2010

FURTHER READING & INTERNET RESOURCES

Books

Cheadle, Don. *Not on Our Watch: The Mission to End Genocide in Darfur and Beyond.* New York: Hyperion, 2007.

Damon, Matt and Ben Affleck. *Good Will Hunting: A Screenplay.* New York: Hyperion, 1997.

Girod, Christina M. *Matt Damon.* San Diego, CA: Lucent Books, 2001.

Greene, Meg. *Matt Damon.* Philadelphia, PA: Chelsea House, 2001.

Wukovits, John. *Ben Affleck.* San Diego, CA: Lucent Books, 2004.

Web Sites

http://movies.yahoo.com/movie/contributor/1800020155
The Yahoo! Movies pages on Matt Damon include a detailed biography, a list of his films, photographs, and links to other websites.

http://www.allmovie.com/artist/matt-damon-p16762
The All Movie Guide pages on Matt Damon include a detailed biography and list of films and awards. The guide also includes detailed pages for individual films, including plot synopses and cast lists.

http://imdb.com/name/nm0000354/
The Internet Movie Database includes 85 video clips of Matt Damon, including movie trailers.

http://movies.aol.com/celebrity/matt-damon/16762/main
Moviefone has an opinionated listing of Matt Damon's 10 best and worst roles, with stills.

Publisher's note:
The Web sites mentioned in this book were active at the time of publication. The publisher is not responsible for Web sites that have changed their addresses or discontinued operation since the date of publication. The publisher will review and update the Web site addresses each time the book is reprinted.

GLOSSARY

amnesia—a loss of memory, usually as a result of shock or injury.

amnesiac—a person with amnesia.

audition—to try out for a part in a performance.

box office—literally, the small office where tickets for a theatrical performance are sold; often used in describing the commercial success or failure of a show or film.

cameo—a brief appearance by a well-known actor in a film.

cinematic—of or dealing with movies; from cinema.

improvised—created or performed without preparation.

mainstream—ideas or thoughts that are considered normal or reflecting commonly held views.

Oscar—nickname for the golden statuette given annually at the Academy Awards by the Academy of Motion Picture Arts and Sciences in recognition of excellence.

paparazzi—a freelance photographer who aggressively pursues celebrities.

premiere—the first public showing of a movie or opening of a performance.

prodigy—a person with unusual abilities, often in math or music.

pseudonym—a false name used by an author, also called a pen name.

screenplay—a script written for a movie or television show.

sequel—a film or book using the characters or situation from an earlier work.

slapstick—comedy based on physical humor.

turnaround—in film production, when a studio decides to sell the rights to a project to another studio; can also refer to the cancellation of a project.

voice-over—piece of narration by a person who is not seen on screen.

NOTES

page 6 "A star is not the . . ." "Matt Damon Receives Star on Hollywood Walk of Fame, " *YouTube*, August 24, 2007 http://www.youtube.com/watch?v=dSxOR1EvpmY.

page 6 "A few times in my life . . ." "Matt Damon Receives Star on Hollywood Walk of Fame, " *YouTube*.

page 6 "Ben and I lived . . ." "Matt Damon Receives Star on Hollywood Walk of Fame, " *YouTube*.

page 8 "George told me people . . ." William Keck, "'Ocean Thirteen' Stars Leave an Imprint at Premiere," *USA Today*, June 6, 2006.

page 9 "You gave an aging suburban . . ." "Don't Call Me Sexy: A Letter from Matt Damon," *People Magazine*, November 26, 2007, p. 72.

page 9 "[It] perfectly demonstrates many of . . ." "Don't Call Me Sexy: A Letter from Matt Damon," *People Magazine*.

page 11 "So growing up for me . . ." Ingrid Sischy, "Matt and Ben—Interview with Matt Damon and Ben Affleck, the Writers and Actors of 'Good Will Hunting,'" *Interview*, December 1997.

page 12 "Because I grew up . . ." Chris Nickson, *Matt Damon: An Unauthorized Biography* (Los Angeles: Renaissance Books, 1999), p. 37.

page 19 "I ate nothing but . . ." Nickson, *Matt Damon*, p. 98.

page 19 "I really wasn't a big . . ." Nickson, *Matt Damon*, p. 99.

page 20 "The day after I . . ." Nickson, *Matt Damon*, p. 115.

page 24 "You start seeing mistakes . . ." Jeff Simon, "Matt Damon, Not Carried Away by the Magic of the Moment," *Buffalo News*, July 26, 1998, p. F1.

page 25 "Project Greenlight was . . ." "Matt Damon: Project Greenlight," *The Oprah Winfrey Show*, http://www.oprah.com/tows/pastshows/tows_2002/tows_past_20020314.jhtml.

page 28 "[I wanted to] try an action movie . . ." Rebecca Ascher-Walsh, "The Hitman Cometh," *Entertainment Weekly*, June 21, 2002, p. 35.

page 28 "Normally, I've played people . . ." Rebecca Ascher-Walsh, "Bourne Again," *Entertainment Weekly*, July 23, 2004.

page 30 "It has had the biggest . . ." Mark Cina, "Matt's Action Off-Screen," *US Weekly*, August 13, 2007, p. 82.

page 33 "I'd go back and . . ." Rebecca Ascher-Walsh, "Bourne Again," *Entertainment Weekly*, July 23, 2004.

page 35 "I'm with a normal girl . . ." "Damon Enjoys Life with 'Civilian' Girlfriend," *World Entertainment News Network*, November 23, 2005.

page 35 "Fame is what . . ." Louis B. Hobson, "Regular Superstar Damon Shuns Entourage Mentality," *Calgary Sun*, July 26, 1998, p. SC2.

page 38 "You remember that movie . . ." Kristina M. Moore, "Damon Returns with 'The Departed,'" *The Harvard Crimson*, October 5, 2006.

page 40 "It was a hard movie . . ." Donna Freydkin, "Matt Damon's Year of Goodwill," *USA Today*, December 14, 2006.

NOTES

page 41 "It's great, great. . . ." "Fatherhood 'Defies Description,'" *People Magazine*, December 11, 2006, http://www.people.com/people/article/0,,1568653,00.html.

page 41 "Having a kid changes you . . ." Alysia Poe, "Shining Stars," *InStyle*, December 2006, p. 364.

page 42 "To see so much hope . . ." "Matt Damon in Africa with ONE," *The ONE Blog*, May 9, 2006, http://www.one.org/blog/2006/05/09/matt-damon-in-africa-with-one/.

page 42 "My friends at the ONE Campaign . . ." "H2O Africa: A Letter from Matt Damon," *Running the Sahara*," http://www.runningthesahara.com/charity.html.

page 45 "The careers I look at . . ." Mark Cina, "Matt's Action Off-Screen," *US Weekly*, August 13, 2007, p. 82.

page 45 "Anybody who has worked with [Matt] . . ." Donna Freydkin. "Matt Damon's Year of Goodwill," *USA Today*, December 14, 2006.

INDEX

Academy Awards, 22, **23**
Affleck, Ben, 6, **10**, 12, **13**, **14**, 15–17, 19–21, **23**, 25, 48
Affleck, Casey, **16**, 31
All the Pretty Horses, **26**, 27

Barroso, Alexia (stepdaughter), 35
Barroso, Luciana Bozan (wife), 9, 33–35, 41, 45, 52
The Bourne Identity, 28–30, 31, 33, 45, 54
The Bourne Supremacy, 33
The Bourne Ultimatum, 5, 6, 40, 41, **44**
The Brothers Grimm, 32–33

Carlsson-Paige, Nancy (mother), 11–12
charity work, 41–44, 54–55
Cheadle, Don, **31**, **40**, 44, 55
Clooney, George, 7–8, 9, 30, **31**, **40**, 44, 45, 55
Coppola, Francis Ford, 20, 49
Courage Under Fire, 18–19, 20, 21, 29

Damon, Isabella (daughter), 41
Damon, Kent (father), 11
Damon, Kyle (brother), 11
Damon, Luciana. *See* Barroso, Luciana Bozan (wife)
Damon, Matt
  awards and honors won by, 8–9, 22, **23**
  birth and childhood, 11–12
  and celebrity, 22, 35
  charity work, 41–44, 54–55
  and *Good Will Hunting,* 15–17, 19–22, **23**, 52
  at Harvard University, 12–15
  and Hollywood Walk of Fame star, **4**, 5–7, **34**

marriage, 33–35, 52
movies, 5, 9, 12, 14–33, 37–40, 45
parenthood, 9, 41, 45
as *People Magazine*'s Sexiest Man Alive, 9
and television, 32
Danes, Claire, 52
De Niro, Robert, 19, 37, 38, **39**, 40
The Departed, **36**, 37–38
DiCaprio, Leonardo, **36**, 38
Dogma, 25
Driver, Minnie, 52

Forbes Celebrity 100, 8–9

Geronimo: An American Legend, 14–15
Gerry, 31, 51
Gilliam, Terry, 32
The Good Shepherd, 38–40, 41
Good Will Hunting, 15–17, 19–22, **23**, 48, 51, 52
Grauman's Chinese Theater, 6–7, 46
Greengrass, Paul, 6, 33, 45

H2O Africa Foundation, 42, **43**, 44, 54
Hollywood Walk of Fame star, **4**, 5–7, **34**

The Legend of Bagger Vance, 27
Liman, Doug, 28, 30, 33
LivePlanet, 25, 42
Lonergan, Kenneth, 45
Ludlum, Robert, 54

Not on Our Watch, 44, 55

Ocean's Eleven, 30, **31**, 33, 45
Ocean's Thirteen, **7**, 40, 55
Ocean's Twelve, 33
ONE campaign, 41–42, 44, 54

People Magazine's Sexiest Man Alive, 9
Pitt, Brad, 7, 9, **31**, **40**, 44, 55
Project Greenlight, 25

The Rainmaker, 20, 21, 22, 49, 52
Redford, Robert, 27, 53
Reiner, Rob, 17
Rounders, 25
Running the Sahara, 42

Saving Private Ryan, 21–22, 50, 52
School Ties, 14, 48
Scorsese, Martin, **36**, 37–38
Smith, Kevin, 20
Soderbergh, Steven, 30, **31**, 45
Spielberg, Stephen, 21–22, 50
Stuck on You, 32, 33
Syriana, 33

The Talented Mr. Ripley, **24**, 25, 29
Thornton, Billy Bob, 27

Van Sant, Gus, 20–21, 31, 51

Washington, Denzel, 18–19
Weinstein, Harvey, 20
Weintraub, Jerry, 7, 44, 55
Wheeler, David, 13
Whitesell, Patrick, 15
Williams, Robin, 20–21, 22, 31
Winfrey, Oprah, 19, 22, **24**, 25, 52

Numbers in **bold italics** refer to captions.

ABOUT THE AUTHOR

Pamela D. Toler is a freelance writer in Chicago, specializing in history and the arts. She has written about ancient Peruvian feather hats, Siberian reindeer hair embroidery, pyramid cults, and the first translation of the Arabian Nights. When she isn't writing about weird stuff, she's watching old movies on cable.

PICTURE CREDITS

page

- **1:** AdMedia/Sipa Press
- **4:** S. Bukley/Shutterstock.com
- **7:** AP Photos
- **8:** Jaguar PS/Shutterstock.com
- **10:** ASP/PRMS
- **13:** AP Photo
- **14:** Paramount Pictures/FilmMagic
- **16:** UPI Photos
- **18:** 20th Century Fox/NMI
- **21:** Miramax/FilmMagic
- **23:** Featureflash/Shutterstock.com
- **24:** Harpo Productions/FPS
- **26:** Miramax/FilmMagic
- **29:** Universal Pictures/NMI
- **31:** Warner Bros./FilmMagic
- **32:** MGM/NMI
- **34:** Jaguar PS/Shutterstock.com
- **36:** Warner Bros./FilmMagic
- **39:** Universal Pictures/NMI
- **40:** Warner Bros./NMI
- **43:** Pepsi-Cola/NMI
- **44:** Joe Seer/Shutterstock.com
- **46:** LOC/NMI
- **47:** T&T/IOA Photos
- **48:** ASP/PRMS
- **49:** Sony Pictures Classics/FilmMagic
- **50:** Helene C, Stikkel/DoD/PRMS
- **51:** IFC Film/Movie Pictures
- **52:** Steve Granitz/WireImage
- **53:** United Artists/NMI
- **55:** Warner Bros./NMI